ENDANGERED AND THREATENED ANIMALS

THE
GRAY WOLF

A MyReportLinks.com Book

Chris Reiter

MyReportLinks.com Books

an imprint of

Enslow Publishers, Inc. E

Box 398, 40 Industrial Road
Berkeley Heights, NJ 07922
USA

MyReportLinks.com Books, an imprint of Enslow Publishers, Inc. MyReportLinks is a trademark of Enslow Publishers, Inc.

Copyright © 2003 by Enslow Publishers, Inc.

Library of Congress Cataloging-in-Publication Data

Reiter, Chris.
    The gray wolf / Chris Reiter.
        p. cm. — (Endangered and threatened animals)
    Summary: Discusses what gray wolves are, why they are endangered, what their current status is, and what is being done to help them. Includes Internet links to Web sites related to gray wolves.
    Includes bibliographical references (p.   ).
    ISBN 0-7660-5056-4
    1. Wolves—Juvenile literature. 2. Endangered species—Juvenile literature. [1. Wolves. 2. Endangered species.] I. Title. II. Series.
QL737.C22 R455 2003
599.773—dc21

                   2002008693

Printed in the United States of America

10 9 8 7 6 5 4 3 2 1

To Our Readers:
Through the purchase of this book, you and your library gain access to the Report Links that specifically back up this book.

The Publisher will provide access to the Report Links that back up this book and will keep these Report Links up to date on **www.myreportlinks.com** for three years from the book's first publication date.

We have done our best to make sure all Internet addresses in this book were active and appropriate when we went to press. However, the author and the Publisher have no control over, and assume no liability for, the material available on those Internet sites or on other Web sites they may link to.

The usage of the MyReportLinks.com Books Web site is subject to the terms and conditions stated on the Usage Policy Statement on **www.myreportlinks.com**.

In the future, a password may be required to access the Report Links that back up this book. The password is found on the bottom of page 4 of this book.

Any comments or suggestions can be sent by e-mail to comments@myreportlinks.com or to the address on the back cover.

Photo Credits: Art Explosion, p. 10; California Wolf Center, pp. 15, 39; © Corel Corporation, pp. 1, 3, 12, 17, 21, 26, 31, 33, 35, 43; Defenders of Wildlife, pp. 29, 41; John Bavaro, p. 19; MyReportLinks.com Books, p. 4; National Wildlife Federation, p. 20; Sinapu, p. 13; Wolf Country, p. 24; Wolf Web, p. 22; U.S. Fish and Wildlife Service, p. 44; Yellowstone National Park, p. 37.

Cover Photo: © Corel Corporation.

Contents

MyReportLinks.com Books
Great Books, Great Links, Great for Research!

MyReportLinks.com Books present the information you need to learn about your report subject. In addition, they show you where to go on the Internet for more information. The pre-evaluated Report Links that back up this book are kept up to date on **www.myreportlinks.com**. With the purchase of a MyReportLinks.com Books title, you and your library gain access to the Report Links that specifically back up that book. The Report Links save hours of research time and link to dozens—even hundreds—of Web sites, source documents, and photos related to your report topic.

Please see "To Our Readers" on the Copyright page for important information about this book, the MyReportLinks.com Books Web site, and the Report Links that back up this book.

Access:

The Publisher will provide access to the Report Links that back up this book and will try to keep these Report Links up to date on our Web site for three years from the book's first publication date. Please enter **EGW1619** if asked for a password.

Report Links

The Internet sites described below can be accessed at
http://www.myreportlinks.com

*EDITOR'S CHOICE

▶ Defenders of Wildlife: Wolves

The Defenders of Wildlife Web site offers a comprehensive overview of wolves. Here you will find general information about wolves, including fact sheets, issues, regional wolf information, and much more.

Link to this Internet site from http://www.myreportlinks.com

*EDITOR'S CHOICE

▶ The Wolf Education and Research Center

Based in Winchester, Idaho, the Wolf Education and Research Center is involved in gray wolf research in both the public and private sectors. Visit Wolf Wisdom for encyclopedic coverage of the gray wolf and its recovery in the Northern Rockies.

Link to this Internet site from http://www.myreportlinks.com

*EDITOR'S CHOICE

▶ Wolves

At the National Geographic Web site you will learn about the gray wolf and its environment, including how the gray wolf is affected by natural forces, droughts, harsh winters, and forest fires.

Link to this Internet site from http://www.myreportlinks.com

*EDITOR'S CHOICE

▶ Gray Wolf Profile

At this Web site you will find information about the gray wolf's diet, habitat, range, primary threats, population restrictions, and other details.

Link to this Internet site from http://www.myreportlinks.com

*EDITOR'S CHOICE

▶ Endangered Species Act

At this Web site you will learn about the Endangered Species Act, how a species becomes endangered, critical habitats, recovery planning, agency actions, and habitat conservation plans.

Link to this Internet site from http://www.myreportlinks.com

*EDITOR'S CHOICE

▶ Wolves

At the Yellowstone National Park Web site you can read an article about the successful reintroduction of wolves into the park. Here you will find maps of the wolf pack territories and brief descriptions of the packs.

Link to this Internet site from http://www.myreportlinks.com

The Internet sites described below can be accessed at
http://www.myreportlinks.com

▶ About Our Zoo: Gray Wolf
The Oregon Zoo offers a brief overview of the gray wolf, outlining the basic
facts about the animal's size, as well as its various adaptations and colorations.
Also covered are the wolf's behavior, life span, diet, and range.

Link to this Internet site from http://www.myreportlinks.com

▶ California Wolf Center
At this Web site you will learn about the California Wolf Center's efforts
to educate and promote conservation of the gray wolf. You will also find a
"Facts . . . Myths . . ." section devoted to wolves.

Link to this Internet site from http://www.myreportlinks.com

▶ Endangered Species Act of 1973
At this Web site you will find the full text of the Endangered Species Act
of 1973.

Link to this Internet site from http://www.myreportlinks.com

▶ Gray Wolf
EnchantedLearning.com offers a fun way for younger students to learn a little
bit about the gray wolf and polish up their coloring skills at the same time.
Print its outline of a wolf and give it to your child or another youngster
to color.

Link to this Internet site from http://www.myreportlinks.com

▶ Gray Wolf: Canus Lupus
Kid's Planet provides a fact sheet on the gray wolf. Here you will find
information about the wolf's status, description, life span, habitat, food,
behavior, and threats.

Link to this Internet site from http://www.myreportlinks.com

▶ International Wolf Center
Based in Ely, Minnesota, the International Wolf Center seeks to ensure the
wolf's continued survival through education. The center's Web site is loaded
with information about wolf biology, management, and behavior.

Link to this Internet site from http://www.myreportlinks.com

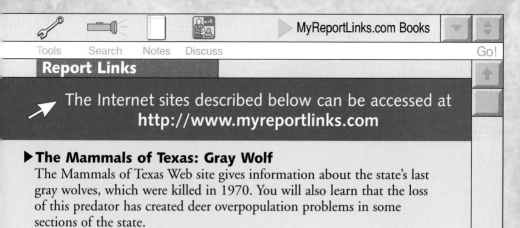
▶ **The Mammals of Texas: Gray Wolf**
The Mammals of Texas Web site gives information about the state's last
gray wolves, which were killed in 1970. You will also learn that the loss
of this predator has created deer overpopulation problems in some
sections of the state.

Link to this Internet site from http://www.myreportlinks.com

▶ **Mexican Gray Wolf (canis lupus balleyi)**
At this Web site you will learn about the Mexican gray wolf's ecological
role, habitat, and progress. This site also offers information about the
Mexican gray wolf packs, including the Bonito Creek pack, the Mule
pack, the Hawk's Nest pack, and many others.

Link to this Internet site from http://www.myreportlinks.com

▶ *Nova:* **Wild Wolves**
Nova, the PBS science show, created this site as an online companion
piece for an episode about the gray wolf. Articles examine the meaning
of the wolf's vocalizations and the importance of the wolf as a predator
in the wild.

Link to this Internet site from http://www.myreportlinks.com

▶ **Profiles in Conservation**
At this Web site you will find a profile of Aldo Leopold. Here you will
learn how Leopold helped to preserve 500,000 acres of New Mexico's
Gila National Forest and his influential writings.

Link to this Internet site from http://www.myreportlinks.com

▶ **Red Wolf Recovery: A Rosy Picture**
This article from Zoogoer, published by Friends of the National Zoo,
reports on the progress of the recovery program for the red wolf. The
species has been reintroduced in portions of North Carolina,
Mississippi, Florida, and South Carolina.

Link to this Internet site from http://www.myreportlinks.com

▶ **Return of the Species**
Beautifully illustrated, this site relates the story of the wolf's successful
reintroduction to the wilderness in and around Yellowstone National
Park. The site looks at some other species as well, including the
trumpeter swan.

Link to this Internet site from http://www.myreportlinks.com

Back	Forward	Stop	Review	Home	Explore	Favorites	History

Report Links

The Internet sites described below can be accessed at
http://www.myreportlinks.com

▶ **The Searching Wolf**

This comprehensive wolf site covers in great detail virtually every aspect of
wolf anatomy and life. In addition to its collection of on-site information,
The Searching Wolf provides a gateway to related resources elsewhere.

Link to this Internet site from http://www.myreportlinks.com

▶ **Southern Rockies Wolf Web**

Sinapu is a grassroots organization working to have the gray wolf reintroduced
to wilderness areas of the Southern Rockies. Its Web site features extensive
information about its campaign and information about the gray wolf.

Link to this Internet site from http://www.myreportlinks.com

▶ **The Wild Habitat: Gray Wolf**

This ThinkQuest site provides a handy profile of the gray wolf, covering
the animal's physical characteristics, habitat, diet, and reproductive behavior.
A separate article covers the successful effort to reintroduce the wolf in
Yellowstone National Park.

Link to this Internet site from http://www.myreportlinks.com

▶ **The Wolf in Alaska**

At the Alaska Department of Fish and Game Web site you will find an
assortment of information about the gray wolf. This includes the Wolf
Conservation and Management Policy for Alaska, the biology of wolves in
Alaska, and the Alexander Archipelago wolf, a subspecies of the gray wolf.

Link to this Internet site from http://www.myreportlinks.com

▶ **Wolf: Canis lupus**

At this Web site you will learn about the height and size of the gray wolf, its
eating habits, adaptations, and distribution. You can also explore an interactive
image of the gray wolf and learn about some of its important features.

Link to this Internet site from http://www.myreportlinks.com

▶ **The Wolf Pack**

This article explores how wolves interact with one another within a pack.
Here you will learn about the heirarchical relationships within a pack and how
they demonstrate their status. You will also learn about the different ways
wolves communicate.

Link to this Internet site from http://www.myreportlinks.com

Report Links

The Internet sites described below can be accessed at
http://www.myreportlinks.com

▶ **Wolves**
Montana Kids Web site provides an overview of the gray wolf. Here you will learn about their habitat, prey, mating cycle, how they communicate, and other interesting facts.

Link to this Internet site from http://www.myreportlinks.com

▶ **Wolves**
At this site you will find a comprehensive overview of wolves in the northern Cascades. You will also find a list of wolf facts, learn about conservation management, and how you can help.

Link to this Internet site from http://www.myreportlinks.com

▶ **Wolves in the North Cascades: Questions and Answers**
This Web site contains a brief overview of wolves living in the North Cascades. A question and answer section teaches about the wolves. Also provided is a brief history of wolves.

Link to this Internet site from http://www.myreportlinks.com

▶ **Wolf Recovery Foundation**
Founded in 1986, the Wolf Recovery Foundation is a nonprofit organization based in Boise, Idaho. The foundation's Web site offers good deal of information about wolves as well as a directory of links to related resources elsewhere online.

Link to this Internet site from http://www.myreportlinks.com

▶ **Wolves in the Upper Great Lakes**
Before reintroduction programs were launched in the West in the 1990s, the last stronghold of the gray wolf in the United States was the Upper Great Lakes. This site provides detailed information about the wolf's status in the region.

Link to this Internet site from http://www.myreportlinks.com

▶ **Wolf Web**
Wolf Web attempts to replace some of the misconceptions about the wolf with facts about this extremely social animal. The site features a number of message forums, a photo gallery, and information on wolf classification and diet.

Link to this Internet site from http://www.myreportlinks.com

Length*
(tip of nose to tip of tail)
Males: 5 to 6 1/2 ft.
        (1.5 to 2 m.)
Females: 4 1/2 to 6 ft.
        (1.4 to 1.8 m.)

Height*
(at the shoulder)
26 to 32 in.
(66 to 82 cm)

Weight*
Males: 70 to 110 pounds
        (31.8 to 49.9 kg.)
Females: 60 to 80 pounds
        (27.2 to 36.2 kg.)

Paw Size*
4 in. (10.2 cm) wide by
5 in. (12.7 cm) long

Life Span
Up to 13 years in the wild;
14 to 15 years in captivity

Pelage
(coat of fur)
Gray, but can also be
black, white, or red

Number of Teeth
42

Breeding Season
February to March

Gestation Period
63 days

Litter Size
Each mother bears 4 to 6
one-pound pups

Current North American Range
Gray wolf:
AK, Canada, ID, MI,
MN, MT, WI, WY

Mexican gray wolf:
AZ and NM

Red wolf:
NC

Pack Size
About 7 in lower 48
states; larger in Canada
and Alaska

Pack Territory Size
25 to 150 sq. miles (41 to
242 sq. km.) in lower 48
states; 300 to 1,000 sq.
miles (453 to 1,610 sq.
km.) in Alaska and
Canada

Travel Speed
5 mph (8 kmph) on average; but can reach speeds
of 40 mph (64.4 kmph)
during chase

Threats to Survival
Persecution by humans;
habitat loss

Figures represent average measurements.

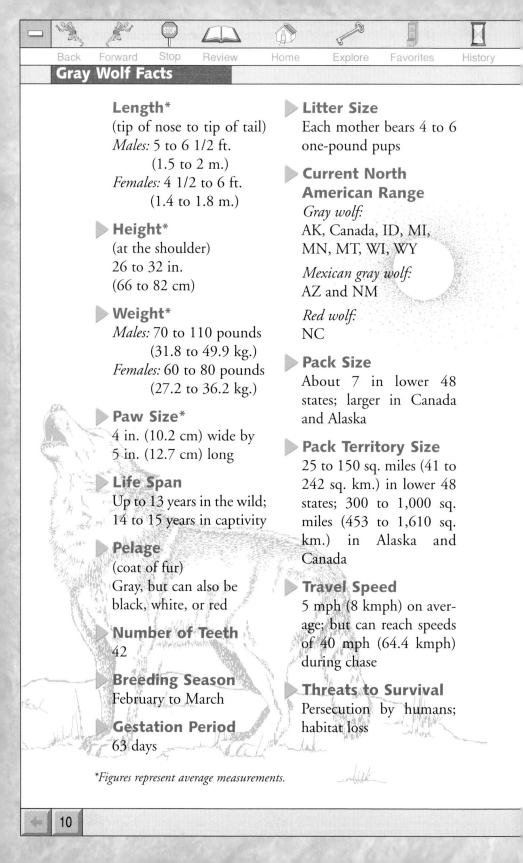

A Chorus of Howls

I climb over a mossy, fallen tree and walk the last few yards to my campsite. I am almost too tired to eat from hiking all day in the foothills of the Alaska Range in Denali National Park. It is a beautiful, wild place. While I set up my tent, the day's last sunlight glows on the paper-white trunks of aspen trees. A moose slurps water on the edge of a nearby lake. A hawk wheels overhead. I want to stop and enjoy the scenery, but all I can think about is kicking off my boots and lying down to rest. After a light snack, I climb into my sleeping bag and bid the moose good night.

From across the lake, a mournful howl pierces the silence. Then another, and another. The loud resounding chorus of howls builds. It is the unmistakable call of a pack of gray wolves. I take a deep breath and lie perfectly still. The calls echo through the forest. They are powerful and eerie. I wonder what the wolves are doing. What is going on out there? I listen for a long time as the forest darkens. I listen long after the last howl has rung through the night, and I fall asleep thinking of wolves.

I am still thinking of wolves long after. When I returned home from my hike, I could not forget the sound of those wild howls. I kept trying to imagine the lives of wolves, and I read stories and studies prepared by people who spent years observing the wolf. I read the accounts of wildlife biologists and storytellers, hunters, and naturalists. Now, when I think of that magical night in the Alaskan wilderness, I can begin to imagine the animals I heard.

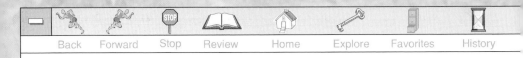

Wolves in the Wild

When I imagine the wolves, I see a pack of seven resting at twilight. They are on the hillside above the lake. There are two full-grown wolves, two young wolves, or yearlings, and three pups. All of the animals have a thick, grayish coat of fur. They are lying close to each other, on their sides, their heads resting on the earth. The pups sleep in a pile; you can hardly tell them apart. A yearling rests with its paw thrown across its long muzzle. The wolves' faces, especially around the eyes and ears, are highlighted with black fur. The eyes of an awakening wolf are deep green.

The wolf rises to his feet and stretches, arching his back and yawning. His yawn shows a mouthful of sharp teeth and large, powerful jaws. His legs are long and his paws enormous. He is the biggest wolf in the pack. From his front paw to the tip of his ears he is 32 inches tall. He weighs about 110 pounds. From his nose to the end of his

Wolves use howling to communicate with one another and keep the pack together physically. Since wolves hunt over long distances to find food, howling helps the pack to regroup.

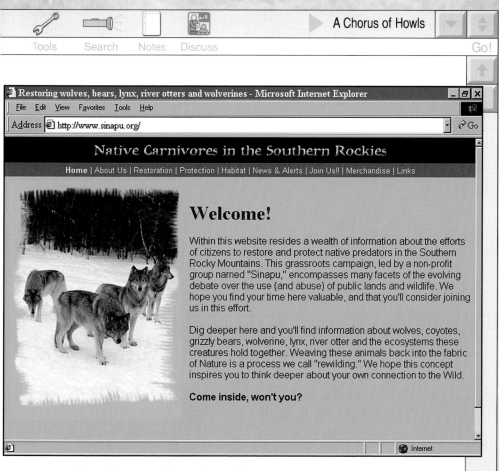

Restoring wolves, bears, lynx, river otters and wolverines - Microsoft Internet Explorer

File   Edit   View   Favorites   Tools   Help

Address http://www.sinapu.org/

Native Carnivores in the Southern Rockies

Home | About Us | Restoration | Protection | Habitat | News & Alerts | Join Us!! | Merchandise | Links

Welcome!

Within this website resides a wealth of information about the efforts of citizens to restore and protect native predators in the Southern Rocky Mountains. This grassroots campaign, led by a non-profit group named "Sinapu," encompasses many facets of the evolving debate over the use (and abuse) of public lands and wildlife. We hope you find your time here valuable, and that you'll consider joining us in this effort.

Dig deeper here and you'll find information about wolves, coyotes, grizzly bears, wolverine, lynx, river otter and the ecosystems these creatures hold together. Weaving these animals back into the fabric of Nature is a process we call "rewilding." We hope this concept inspires you to think deeper about your own connection to the Wild.

Come inside, won't you?

Internet

▲ *Wolves typically travel in packs to hunt more effectively.*

long, fluffy tail, he measures 6 1/2 feet.[1] He is the leader, the alpha male, of this pack of wolves.

After a good stretch, he raises his nose skyward and howls. The other wolves stir. They stand and stretch. A yearling howls, and then the other joins in. The leader's mate, the alpha female, howls too. Before long, two other wolves run from the woods and join the pack. The chorus of howls rings through the forest. Then the wolves gather around the alpha male. They push their noses into him and lick his face. The group nuzzles together, and after much tail wagging and woofing, they break apart. They are ready for a night of hunting.

On a typical hunt, wolves may run from 20 to 40 miles in a single evening. Traveling in a pack, they lope along in a steady trot, ranging over vast territory in search of food. Wolves prey on animals bigger than themselves. They hunt moose and elk, deer and caribou, and they almost always hunt together. A single wolf could probably catch and kill a deer on its own, but cooperative hunting is a much more reliable way of securing a meal.

▶ The Big, Bad Wolf

Humans have often seen the wolf's hunting prowess as a terrible threat. Yet, there is no record of a healthy wild wolf killing a human in America. Wolves do not prey on humans. Many people have feared wolves because of stories that exaggerate the "wildness" of wolves. In medieval Europe, for instance, tales and fables linked wolves with the devil or cast them as evil werewolves.[2] Today we are all familiar with stories of "the big, bad wolf."

When European settlers came to North America, they dreaded the wolves they saw near their new farms and villages. They worried that wolves would eat their pigs, cows, and horses. Many settlers began hunting the animals. By the end of the 1800s, few wolves survived in the eastern United States.

As settlers moved across the continent, they continued to hunt wolves. Some hunters were paid to kill wolves. Others hunted wolves for their coats of thick fur. One naturalist estimates that up to 2 million wolves were killed in the American West.[3] By the middle of the twentieth century, only a small number of wolves survived in the United States. They lived far away from cities and towns. They survived only in the wild lands of northern Minnesota, on an island wilderness in Lake Michigan, and in Alaska.

Saving an Endangered Species

Things began to look up for the wolf in 1973. That is when the U.S. Congress passed the Endangered Species Act. The law declared that all species of plants and animals that were near extinction should be protected from harm. A species is near extinction when its population is very low. It is in danger of disappearing from the earth forever. There were so few wolves left in the lower forty-eight states that the wolf was in danger of extinction. When the Endangered Species Act became law, the gray wolf, the red

http://www.californiawolfcenter.org/images/wolves/wolf1.jpg - Microsoft Internet Explorer

File Edit View Favorites Tools Help

Address http://www.californiawolfcenter.org/images/wolves/wolf1.jpg   Go

Done   Internet

▲ The Mexican gray wolf, pictured here, was listed as endangered in 1973, the year Congress passed the Endangered Species Act. Since then, several recovery plans have been developed to restore the Mexican gray wolf to its natural habitat.

wolf, and the Mexican gray wolf, a subspecies of gray wolf, were listed as endangered.

The Endangered Species Act also directs the United States government to help each endangered species recover. The U.S. Fish and Wildlife Service (USFWS) is the government agency that develops recovery plans. Sometimes they help species recover by bringing them back to the places where they used to live. After years of study, the agency decided to help gray wolves return to their former home in the northern Rocky Mountains.

In 1995, USFWS wildlife biologists, cooperating with the Canadian government, captured gray wolves in Canada and brought them to Yellowstone National Park. Would the wolves get used to their new home? Would they thrive in Yellowstone? Would they run back to Canada? No one knew.

Many people hoped the wolves would stay. They had been waiting for the day when wolves would once again run, hunt, and howl in the Rocky Mountains. As the wolves were brought to Yellowstone, they crossed their fingers and hoped.

The Social Hunter

Before Europeans settled in what is now the United States, wolves ranged across all of North America. From Canada to Mexico and from the Atlantic Coast to the western mountain ranges, wolf packs roamed the continent. The gray wolf lived in the deep northern forests, on the prairie, and in the western mountains. In the South, red wolves wandered the woods and wetlands. The Mexican gray wolf hunted in the dry highlands of Arizona and New Mexico.

▲ *The red wolf was once abundant in the Southeastern United States.*

Wolves thrived in so many places because they were very good hunters. Like Alaskan gray wolves, the wolves that lived in New England, Iowa, North Carolina, and Wyoming hunted large animals. They hunted deer, elk, and buffalo. They were very good at it. The wolf was North America's most successful big game predator.

What makes wolves such good hunters? Scientists say that preying on large mammals is the wolf's role in nature. They call the wolf's role its niche. Over millions of years, each kind of animal, or species, has learned how to play its role. Generation by generation, animal species adapt to their roles and their surroundings. A tree swallow has feathers and wings to fly and a beak to catch insects. Trout have gills for breathing and strong, sleek bodies for swimming in the currents of a creek. Each animal is built to survive and prosper.

Wolves are built for hunting big game. Their sense of smell, for example, is one hundred times more sensitive than that of humans. Wolves can smell an elk herd a mile away. Their long-legged bodies are perfect for running fast and far. They can bound 16 feet, sprint up to 40 miles per hour, and maintain a chase for twenty minutes. Then there is the wolf's powerful bite. Wolves can tear through the thick hide of a running moose. They can hold their prey with a vise-like grip. Biologist David Mech once watched a wolf cling by its teeth to the nose of a moose. The wolf held on even as the moose's swinging head lifted the wolf off the ground.[1]

▶ Life in a Wolf Pack

These physical traits make each wolf a powerful hunter. Although, as we saw with the Alaskan wolves, hunting in packs is the real key to wolf survival. In fact, the pack

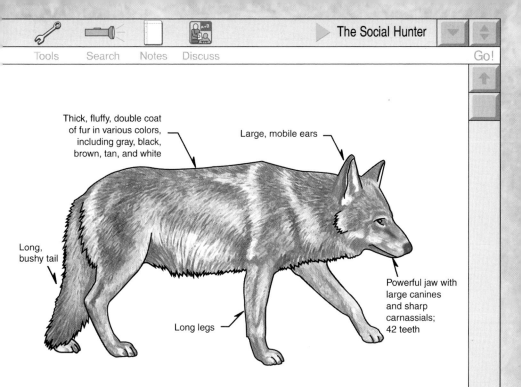

Thick, fluffy, double coat of fur in various colors, including gray, black, brown, tan, and white

Large, mobile ears

Long, bushy tail

Powerful jaw with large canines and sharp carnassials; 42 teeth

Long legs

shapes the entire life of the wolf. Wolves not only hunt together; they live, travel, feed, and rest together, too.

It can be hard to imagine such fierce hunters getting along well enough to live in packs. Wolves, however, can be as playful as they are ferocious. Naturalist Barry Lopez has watched wolves play games with ravens.[2] Wolf biologist Adolph Murie observed that wolves show great friendliness toward each other.[3]

This friendliness is the glue that binds the pack into a family. It begins just after birth, when wolf pups cuddle with their mothers and fathers. As the wolves mature, other adult wolves play with the young and teach them to hunt. Sometimes adults will even baby-sit when a new mother leaves her pups to go hunting with the rest of the pack. When the pack returns, the pups will touch their lips to the mouths of the adults. The adults then regurgitate a meal of fresh meat. The pups also wrestle and romp

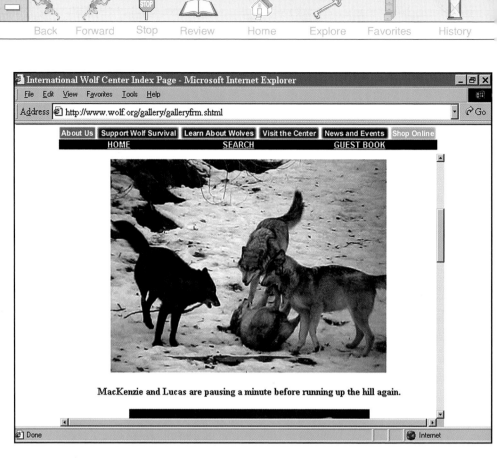

▲ *Although they are ferocious hunters, wolves are actually very playful animals. Their playfulness is an important part of keeping the pack together.*

together. As they grow, they will continue to greet each other with affection. They often will play together and share food.

The wolf pack also has family rules. A strong, dominant wolf leads the pack. This dominant wolf is known as the alpha male or alpha female. The other wolves in the pack are usually family members. They follow the alpha's lead. An alpha female, for example, may be the pack's most skilled, resourceful hunter. She may guide the pack to a herd of deer. She may also choose the animal that the pack will attack. Her leadership wins the respect of the rest of the pack. They help her raise her pups. They eat after she has had her fill. Each wolf knows its role in the pack.

▶ The Language of the Wolf

The roles and family bonds of the pack create a "wolf society." Like human society, wolf society is held together by communication. Just as we talk, shake hands, and write, wolves have distinct ways of expressing themselves. Along with nuzzling and howling before a hunt, wolves communicate with a variety of postures, sounds, and expressions. They bark or growl to display their strength. They squeak to show affection. The wolf's expressive face reveals emotions from interest and amazement to suspicion.

The wolf's body sends signals, too. Holding the tail high in the air communicates self-confidence. Sometimes the alpha wolf lays its chin across another wolf's back. Without a growl or a fight, it shows that the alpha is in charge. Wolves also send messages to each other by scratching the ground or urinating in specific places. These "scent marks" show the way to a hunting trail or mark the boundaries of their territory. All of these signs and gestures create a language that each wolf understands. This language keeps the pack together.

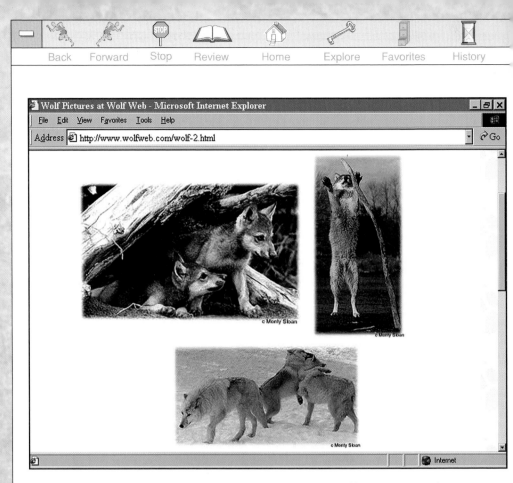

▲ This collage of photos shows the gray wolf at different stages in the "wolf society." Wolf pups are taught from the time they are young to show affection. As they grow into mature wolves, they maintain this friendliness with others in the pack.

By sharing the language of the hunting pack, wolves ensure their survival in the wild. Unfortunately, the wolf has not been well understood by most humans. Some people have honored the wolf for its intelligence, endurance, and strength. Yet many have seen the wolf as a bloodthirsty demon they must destroy. The Europeans who settled the Americas most often saw the demon. When the Europeans first came to North America, the wolf faced its greatest challenge.

Threats Old and New

Living in the wild, wolves face many challenges. Hunting is a difficult way to make a living. Wolves must run miles each day to find a meal. Capturing prey is dangerous. A moose's powerful kick can break a wolf's leg or fracture its skull. A headlong dash after a deer through forest thickets sometimes causes injury. Even the strongest wolf does not win every fight with the big animals it pursues. Sometimes wolves are preyed upon. Wolf pups, if left alone, are an easy catch for a bear or a fox.

Wolves must also survive the changing seasons. Summer may bring drought and long runs to watering holes. Winter usually brings cold, harsh storms. Many wolves live in the Far North where temperatures drop well below freezing. Even when snow piles up by the foot, wolves must stay warm and hunt. While bears hibernate and humans sit by warming fires, wolves are out loping through deep snow looking for their next meal.

Faced with all these challenges, wolves survived and flourished for centuries. Still, wolves have just barely survived their greatest challenge: their long, often troubled relationship with humans.

▶ Wolves and Humans

The relationship between wolves and humans goes back millions of years. Ancient hunters competed with wolves for game. Shepherds cautiously have guarded their flocks of sheep from preying wolves. Farmers, too, have kept a

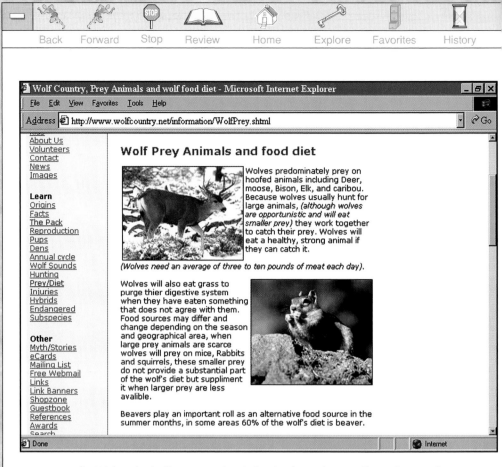

About Us
Volunteers
Contact
News
Images

Learn
Origins
Facts
The Pack
Reproduction
Pups
Dens
Annual cycle
Wolf Sounds
Hunting
Prey/Diet
Injuries
Hybrids
Endangered
Subspecies

Other
Myth/Stories
eCards
Mailing List
Free Webmail
Links
Link Banners
Shopzone
Guestbook
References
Awards
Search

Wolf Prey Animals and food diet

Wolves predominately prey on hoofed animals including Deer, moose, Bison, Elk, and caribou. Because wolves usually hunt for large animals, *(although wolves are opportunistic and will eat smaller prey)* they work together to catch their prey. Wolves will eat a healthy, strong animal if they can catch it.

(Wolves need an average of three to ten pounds of meat each day).

Wolves will also eat grass to purge thier digestive system when they have eaten something that does not agree with them. Food sources may differ and change depending on the season and geographical area, when large prey animals are scarce wolves will prey on mice, Rabbits and squirrels, these smaller prey do not provide a substantial part of the wolf's diet but suppliment it when larger prey are less avalible.

Beavers play an important roll as an alternative food source in the summer months, in some areas 60% of the wolf's diet is beaver.

Done   Internet

▲ *Wolves typically prey on hoofed animals, such as caribou, deer, and moose. Smaller prey might include squirrels or rabbits.*

watchful eye on the woods at the edge of their fields. A pack of hungry wolves could easily eat all of the farmer's pigs or chickens. Without their livestock, the farmer's livelihood would be lost.

Such threats caused most people to hate and fear wolves. These fears became part of the stories people told about the wolf. During the Middle Ages in Europe, for example, the wolves that appeared in fables and poems were liars and thieves. Peasants called famine "the wolf." The Roman Church taught that the wolf was a companion to the devil and that evil "werewolves" roamed the towns of Europe. Most people believed the stories of the day.[1]

When Europeans came to North America, they brought with them their European customs. They brought their trades, their religious beliefs, and their attitudes about life as they saw it. Upon settling in the New World, they found a fruitful land—and a land of many wolves. Just as in Europe, many settlers thought the wolves were sinister. They also feared the surrounding wilderness and felt the need to protect their livestock and their families. When wolves wandered near their new farms and towns, settlers often killed them.

The wolf hunts went beyond mere protection. Wolves were hunted in the wilderness, too. They were pursued in the deep forests. They were killed in the mountains. Sometimes, hunters were paid for killing wolves. In New England, settlers were given as much as one month's salary for each wolf they killed.[2] By the end of the nineteenth century, there were no more wolves in the Northeastern United States.

▶ Conquering the West

Sadly, the process repeated itself wherever settlers traveled in North America. As they moved west, the wolves disappeared. By 1850, explorers, trappers, and homesteaders had begun to reach the Great Plains. There, the wolf had thrived for centuries hunting the great herds of buffalo that roamed the prairie. Wolves preyed on only a tiny fraction of the buffalo herds. They killed what they needed to survive. The buffalo hunters, however, slaughtered almost all the existing herds. Between 1850 and 1880, they killed about 75 million buffalo.[3]

▲ *A herd of bison roaming in Yellowstone National Park.*

Without buffalo to eat, the wolves of the plains turned to livestock. Ranchers had begun to raise cattle in the West, and now they felt the need to protect their herds. They hired men to hunt the wolves that threatened their cattle. With traps and poison, the hunters pursued wolves across the prairie. Sometimes the hunters would set out poisoned animal carcasses for the wolves to eat. Bears, eagles, and foxes also died from eating the poisoned meat.

In 1884, the governments of western states and territories began to pay hunters to kill wolves. Beef had become a staple of the American diet. Cattle ranching had become big business. In Montana, the state government offered a bounty, or payment, to wolf hunters. Hundreds of men tried to make a living hunting wolves. Many made a tidy sum. Between 1883 and 1918, the hunters were paid $342,764 for killing 80,730 wolves.[4]

Even the United States government participated in wolf hunting. Many ranchers grazed their cattle on federal land owned and managed by the government. The ranchers thought the government should provide them with hunters to protect their herds from wolves. In 1915, the U.S. Congress agreed. It passed a law providing money to hire government hunters to kill wolves on federal lands. The government hunters killed nearly twenty-five thousand wolves.[5] Many wolves were hunted and killed in our national parks.

Further west, in the Rocky Mountains and the Cascade Range, wolves were hunted for their fur, or pelts. Hunters with the Hudson's Bay Company, for example, trapped wolves in the North Cascades. Between 1827 and 1859, buyers bought nearly eight thousand pelts there from local trappers.[6] Government hunters were also involved in trapping wolves in the western mountains.

The last of the bounty programs ended in 1965. By then, wolves had been virtually eliminated from the lower forty-eight states. Even in Yellowstone Park there were no wolves. A population of only a few hundred survived in the deep forests of northern Minnesota. A much smaller population held out on Isle Royale, an island wilderness in Lake Michigan.

▶ Hope on the Horizon

The Endangered Species Act has protected wolves since 1973. The act's recovery programs have done much to reverse the harm done to wolves in the United States. Today, the wolf still faces great threats. The rapid growth of our cities and towns continues to consume much of the

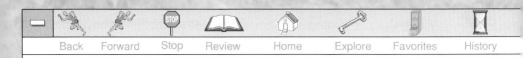
wolf's former range. Feelings toward wolves run deep. Many people still fear and hate them. Despite the protections of the Endangered Species Act, wolves continue to be trapped, even shot.

Yet there is hope. Attitudes can evolve. Feelings can change. It was just a few years between the end of bounty programs and passage of the Endangered Species Act. Citizens' and scientists' image of the wolf changed from evil predator to fellow creature. They began to view the wolf as a creature of strength and intelligence. What had happened? What was the source of this new understanding and concern? What influenced this dramatic change? Surprisingly, it began with a man who hunted wolves.

A Fierce Green Fire

During the days of the wolf hunts, few hunters turned down the chance to shoot at wolves. Many thought that wolves would eat all the deer they loved to hunt. One of those hunters was a man named Aldo Leopold. From 1909 to 1918, Leopold worked for the U.S. Forest Service in the mountains of Arizona and New Mexico. On his rounds

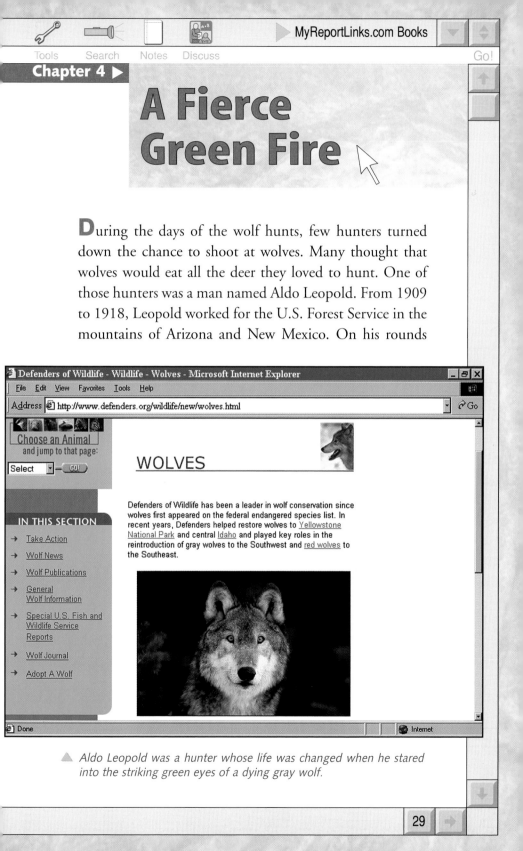

Defenders of Wildlife - Wildlife - Wolves - Microsoft Internet Explorer

File   Edit   View   Favorites   Tools   Help

Address ⌕ http://www.defenders.org/wildlife/new/wolves.html   ⌕ Go

Choose an Animal
and jump to that page:

Select ▾ — GO!

WOLVES

Defenders of Wildlife has been a leader in wolf conservation since wolves first appeared on the federal endangered species list. In recent years, Defenders helped restore wolves to Yellowstone National Park and central Idaho and played key roles in the reintroduction of gray wolves to the Southwest and red wolves to the Southeast.

IN THIS SECTION

→ Take Action

→ Wolf News

→ Wolf Publications

→ General
   Wolf Information

→ Special U.S. Fish and
   Wildlife Service
   Reports

→ Wolf Journal

→ Adopt A Wolf

Done   Internet

▲ Aldo Leopold was a hunter whose life was changed when he stared into the striking green eyes of a dying gray wolf.

one day, he and a group of his fellow rangers saw a pack of wolves. They watched a mother wolf swim across a stream and greet her pups. The rangers shot all the wolves. They thought it was their job to protect the herds of deer for other hunters.

However, when Aldo Leopold approached the dying wolves, he was forever changed. He arrived at the mother wolf's side "in time to watch a fierce green fire dying in her eyes."[1] The "green fire" was the wolf's strong life force. Leopold saw life in the eyes of the wolf. Seeing the wolf up close made him realize that she was a fellow living creature. The wolf's life was different from his own, but honorable. He also understood that the wolf belonged in the mountains. The mountains were the wolf's home and should always be.

▶ A Community of Creatures

Leopold never shot another wolf. Instead he began to study wolves. He found that wolves really did have a place in the mountains. They played an important role in the wilderness. He saw that as wolves live their lives hunting big game, they help keep the wilderness healthy.[2] Wolves preying on deer, for example, often take the less healthy animals. This keeps the surviving herd lean and strong.

When wolves are killed off, the deer herd suffers. Without wolves "trimming" the herd, it grows too large. Then, plants that the deer feed on grow scarce. Imagine cooking dinner for a family of four and then having four extra guests arrive at the last minute. If this continued night after night, the cupboards would soon be bare. That is what happens in the mountains and forests when there are too many deer. There is just not enough food to go around. After awhile, all the deer go hungry. The struggle for food hurts the entire herd.

This is what Aldo Leopold observed in the mountains of Arizona. He saw that wolves, deer, and plants need each other for survival. He recognized they are part of a community. It was a new idea. Most people still believed wolves had no value and should be controlled at all costs. Leopold, though, spoke out. He encouraged people to see that they too lived in nature's community. He asked people to treat the wolf as a community member. Just as we try to love and respect our neighbors, he said, we must try to love and respect wild creatures and wild places.

▶ Adolph Murie and The Toklat Wolves

The biologist Adolph Murie understood Aldo Leopold's ideas. Murie studied wolves on the East Fork of the Toklat

▲ Wolves hunt in packs. They can usually kill a large animal in only a few minutes.

River in Alaska. Like Leopold, Adolph Murie was interested in how wolves help keep the wilderness healthy. He was interested in the relationship between predator and prey. He wanted to know how wolves and Dall sheep lived in the natural community of the Alaskan tundra. Murie spent nearly three years tracking and watching wolves. He hiked, camped out, and spent many hours observing the wolf's habits.

Nearly every day Murie watched and took notes. Over time he came to know a pack of wolves that lived near the Toklat River in Mount McKinley National Park. He noticed that each wolf had a personality. He watched wolves hunt; he listened to them howl. He noted how much they played and how they expressed their feelings for one another. Murie's own feelings for the wolves grew strong. He filled his notebooks with descriptions and stories.

American Indians had always watched wolves as Murie did. They were keen observers of the wolf's behavior. Few European Americans had taken the time to know the wolf in this way. Few had feelings of affection for wolves. Murie later used his Alaska field notes to write a book. He called it *The Wolves of Mount McKinley*. People read Murie's book with great interest. They had never before read such a vivid account of the wolf. Many followed in Murie's footsteps and visited Alaska to observe wolves. Others began to imagine wolves differently. When they thought of wolves, they pictured interesting, appealing creatures, not sinister demons.

Scientists, too, began to show more interest. Murie's report was the first true scientific study of wolf behavior. Many followed, supporting Leopold's and Murie's observations. They found that the wolf was indeed a

Tools   Search   Notes   Discuss .

Go!

▲ Wolves mate during the winter. The female gives birth in a sheltered area called a den.

crucial part of the natural community.[3] Scientists saw that other animals benefited from wolves. Foxes, bears, wolverines, and ravens feed on the remains of animals killed by wolves. As Leopold noted, wolves keep deer and elk herds from getting too big. In the presence of wolves, herd animals have learned to be alert and fast.[4]

Most scientists who studied wolves began to call for their protection. Many citizens did as well. They joined groups devoted to preserving nature and wildlife. Together, the wolf's advocates worked to save it from extinction. Slowly, the stage was being set for the protection of the wolf in North America.

▶ The Endangered Species Act

The wolf was not the only animal that scientists and citizens were concerned about. By the early 1960s, the development of North America was threatening many species. Logging, mining, fishing, and manufacturing had made the United States one of the richest nations on earth. Those industries had also disturbed the land and water that supported American wildlife. There were few grizzly bears in the west. Gray whales were vanishing from the sea. The bald eagle, the symbol of the nation's vitality, was also threatened. Some animals, such as the Carolina parakeet, were already extinct.

Faced with these losses, Americans began to try to save the natural world. Voters urged the United States government to act. In the 1960s and early 1970s, Congress passed laws to protect clean air and water. It acted to control the use of pesticides and to preserve wilderness. Then, in 1973, Congress passed the Endangered Species Act (ESA).

The ESA is designed to protect both threatened and endangered species. Endangered means a species, such as the wolf, is in danger of extinction. Threatened means a species is likely to become endangered in the foreseeable future. The wolf is currently listed as endangered in all but one of the lower forty-eight states. It is listed as threatened in Minnesota.

The Endangered Species Act protects threatened and endangered species in several ways. It forbids hunting, capturing, or harming endangered animals. It calls for the preservation of the lands and waters where endangered species live.[5] Some habitats, or areas in which some endangered species live, for example, have been declared wildlife refuges. On a refuge, a species should never be harmed.

▲ *In 1995, gray wolves were brought to Yellowstone National Park (pictured here). Biologists hoped they could restore the wolf population.*

All these protections are important. They support the core purpose of the ESA, which is to restore endangered species to health. For the gray wolf, a return to health would mean the return of packs of strong, thriving wolves to some of the places where they used to live. Yellowstone National Park and the Idaho Rockies are two such places. In 1995, that is just what happened: the wolf was returned to the western wilderness.

The Return of the Wolf

Yellowstone National Park is the world's first national park. It was established in 1872 to protect the wild forests and mountains of western Wyoming. At 2.2 million acres, Yellowstone is one of the biggest parks in the nation. It is bigger than the states of Rhode Island and Delaware combined.[1]

When land is protected in a park it means that people have agreed to put nature first. In a national park, the forests cannot be cut down, and mines cannot be dug in the mountains. This preserves the natural world. It makes a park a nice place to visit. Many people like to go to parks to hike and camp. Many visit parks to enjoy the wildlife and the scenery.

In Yellowstone National Park, much of the land is the same as it was hundreds, even thousands of years ago. In many of Yellowstone's high mountain valleys, there are no cars and no buildings. Just trees, streams, and wild animals. Lots of wild animals. There are grizzly bears, elk, and beaver. There are lynx, eagles, and trout.

For much of the twentieth century, however, there were no wolves. In 1935, the last wolves were killed in Yellowstone. For years while the other wild animals thrived, the wolves were absent. It was as if one piece of a beautiful handmade quilt was missing. It was as if someone was missing from a family photo. The wolf was the only missing piece of the natural community of Yellowstone. Many people hoped for the wolf's return.

A Wolf Recovery Plan

Hope turned into action when the Endangered Species Act became law. The act gave the U.S. Fish and Wildlife Service the authority to assist the wolf's recovery. The biologists who worked for the service began to plan for the wolf's return. The wild country of Yellowstone offered a perfect setting. The wolf had once thrived in Yellowstone. There were few people, lots of space, and plenty of big game for the wolves to hunt.

Just how would the biologists get wolves back to Yellowstone? Few wolves were living nearby. They would have to capture wild wolves where they were plentiful.

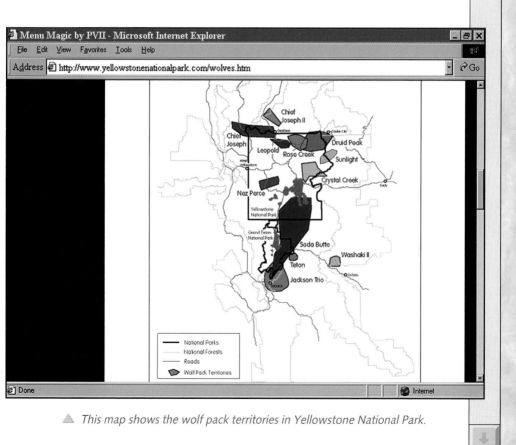

▲ This map shows the wolf pack territories in Yellowstone National Park.

By late winter 1995, with cooperation of the Canadian government, the biologists had begun to capture wolves in Canada. From helicopters, they shot the wolves with darts that made them go to sleep. The wolves were then brought to Yellowstone and released into large outdoor pens. Here the wolves recovered from their long journey. They were freed to roam Yellowstone's wilderness after taking time to get used to their new surroundings.

Fourteen wolves were brought to Yellowstone from Canada in 1995. The wolves were members of many different packs. Each wolf was assigned to a family, or pack, and released into one of the three pens. The pens were about five to ten miles apart. When each pack was released into the wild, it would need lots of space to run and hunt. The biologists named the packs after nearby landmarks where the pens had been situated. There was the Crystal Creek pack, the Rose Creek pack, and the Soda Butte pack.

As the wolves got used to Yellowstone, the biologists watched them from a distance. They only approached the pens to feed elk meat to the wolves. When they saw that the wolves were healthy, they opened the gates to their pens. At first, the wolves did not leave the pens. They were shy and afraid. Soon, one by one, the wolves ran into the wilderness.

Each pack had a different personality. The Crystal Creek pack was cautious and shy. They were careful hunters and did not roam far. The Soda Butte pack was bold. They were quick to explore the canyons of Soda Butte Creek and were fearless hunters. The Rose Creek wolves were a small pack led by a magnificent pair. The two were from different packs in Canada. Both were big, strong, beautiful wolves. They were introduced to each other in the Yellowstone pen. They liked each other very much. They groomed each other and howled together. One observer called the Rose Creek wolves the "romantics."[2]

Before too long, the wolves had settled into Yellowstone. They ran in the forests and drank from the creeks. They ran in the mountain valleys, exploring their new homes. Each pack found places to hunt. They played together and chased elk. At dusk, their howls rang through the mountains. It was a sound that had not been heard in Yellowstone for sixty years.

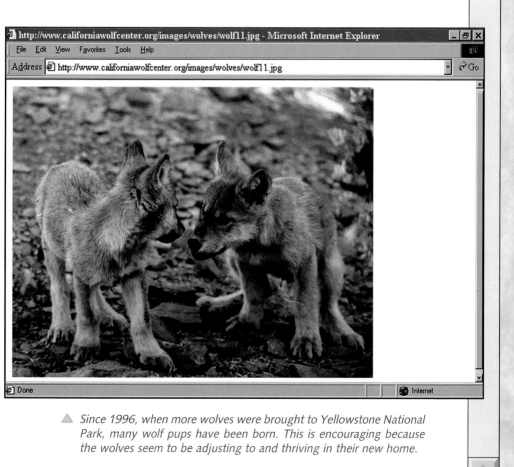

http://www.californiawolfcenter.org/images/wolves/wolf11.jpg - Microsoft Internet Explorer

File   Edit   View   Favorites   Tools   Help

Address http://www.californiawolfcenter.org/images/wolves/wolf11.jpg   Go

Done   Internet

▲ Since 1996, when more wolves were brought to Yellowstone National Park, many wolf pups have been born. This is encouraging because the wolves seem to be adjusting to and thriving in their new home.

More wolves were brought to Yellowstone in 1996. By the spring of 1997, there were nine packs of wolves. Thirteen females from those packs mated and bore sixty-four pups. By July 2000, there were more than 250 wolves in Yellowstone and the central Idaho wilderness.[3] Wolf recovery was going well. The wolves seemed to be thriving in their new home. The biologists from the U.S. Fish and Wildlife Service were pleased. "This is truly an endangered species success story," said Service Director Jamie Rappaport Clark.[4] The wolf was back. The Yellowstone quilt was now complete.

The reintroduction of wolves has had a major impact on the ecosystem of Yellowstone. Grizzly bears, elk, coyotes, eagles, ravens, badgers, foxes, and rodents have all been affected. By reoccupying their long vacant niche as top predator, the wolf has helped restore an equilibrium, or balance, in the biological community. Large plant eaters like moose and elk tend to overgraze and ravage vegetation when herds become too large. Left unchecked the herds then suffer periodic starvation—nature's alternative to the wolves thinning the herds. The reintroduction of the wolf into Yellowstone has benefited vegetation and large plant eaters.[5]

Wolves on the Rebound

Wolves are on the rebound in several places in the United States. As early as 1985, a small pack of wolves migrated into Glacier National Park in Montana from Canada and reproduced the following year.[6] Wolves may never return to their entire former range, but the wolf population continues to recover. In some states wolves have returned on their own. In Minnesota, for example, wolves were never completely killed off. There, the wolf population is growing. Fewer than one thousand wolves lived in Minnesota in the early 1970s. Today there are nearly 2,500. In nearby Wisconsin and Michigan's Upper Peninsula, wolf populations are estimated at 248 and 216, respectively.[7] Wolves have returned to Montana and Idaho, too. Some have traveled there from Yellowstone. Others have migrated from Canada.

Many people hope Canadian wolves will also cross the border into the Northeast. In northern Maine, New Hampshire, Vermont, and New York, the United States–Canadian border is wild country. Once cut to the ground, the forests of the Northeast are growing back. The

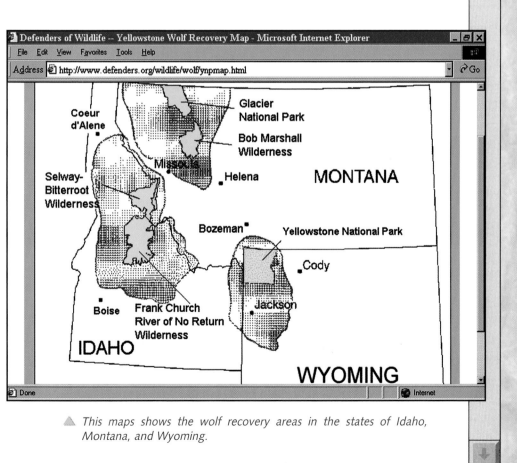

This maps shows the wolf recovery areas in the states of Idaho, Montana, and Wyoming.

land is beginning to resemble the place that wolves once called home. Biologists believe it is now a good place for the animals. They think wolves may soon begin to find their way back to the Northeast from the wild lands of Canada.

As in Yellowstone, the U.S. Fish and Wildlife Service has tried to help wolves when they could not return to their old homes on their own. In the Southeast, the USFWS saved the endangered red wolf. In 1975, there were fewer than fifty red wolves living in the wild.[8] Biologists captured the remaining wolves to protect them from harm. In captivity, the red wolves bred and increased their numbers. In 1987, they were returned to the wild in North Carolina's Alligator River National Wildlife Refuge. The animals were later released into Pocosin Lakes National Wildlife Refuge. Today, there are about a hundred red wolves living in the North Carolina wilderness. Their numbers are slowly growing.

Wolves have also been released in the Southwest. In the 1980s, five Mexican gray wolves were captured and bred in captivity until there were 175 wolves. In 1998, three packs of Mexican gray wolves totaling thirteen were reintroduced into Arizona's Apache National Forest. The following year twenty-one wolves were released. These reintroductions were part of a captive breeding program to prevent extinction of this subspecies. Biologists from the U.S. Fish and Wildlife Service expect the packs to grow and separate into new packs. Before long, they hope, up to a hundred wolves will be living in Arizona's desert wilderness.[9]

Carefully, the biologists have kept track of the wolves as they roam the dry, forested high country. Some of them may remember that the wolves are wandering in the very place Aldo Leopold saw the "fierce green fire" in the eyes of a mother wolf. They must feel proud that they have

▲ *Biologists expect that the gray wolf will thrive in its new environment after it is released from captivity.*

tried to help save the animal that Leopold came to love. Now the wolf is running wild in its homeland. Now the wolf's howl can be heard ringing through the canyons. It is a sound that would make Aldo Leopold thankful. It is a sound that would make him rejoice.

This series is based on the Endangered and Threatened Wildlife list compiled by the U.S. Fish and Wildlife Service (USFWS). Each book explores an endangered or threatened animal, tells why it has become endangered or threatened, and explains the efforts being made to restore the species' population.

The United States Fish and Wildlife Service, in the Department of the Interior, and the National Marine Fisheries Service, in the Department of Commerce, share responsibility for administration of the Endangered Species Act.

In 1973, Congress took the farsighted step of creating the Endangered Species Act, widely regarded as the world's strongest and most effective wildlife conservation law. It set an ambitious goal: to reverse the alarming trend of human-caused extinction that threatened the ecosystems we all share.

The complete list of Endangered and Threatened Wildlife and Plants can be found at
http://endangered.fws.gov/wildlife.html#Species

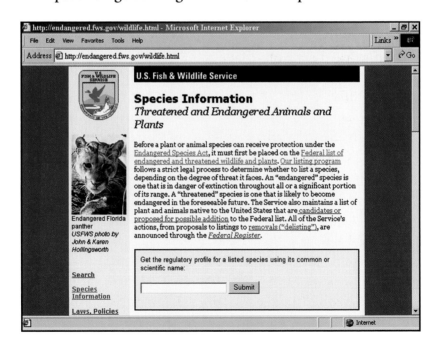

Chapter Notes

Chapter 1. A Chorus of Howls

1. L. David Mech, *The Wolf: The Ecology and Behavior of an Endangered Species* (Minneapolis: University of Minnesota Press, 1981), pp. 11–12.

2. Barry Holstun Lopez, *Of Wolves and Men* (New York: Simon & Schuster, 1978), pp. 140–145.

3. Ibid., p. 180.

Chapter 2. The Social Hunter

1. L. David Mech, *The Wolf: The Ecology and Behavior of an Endangered Species* (Minneapolis: University of Minnesota Press, 1981), pp. 13–15.

2. Barry Holstun Lopez, *Of Wolves and Men* (New York: Simon & Schuster, 1978), pp. 67–68.

3. Adolph Murie, *The Wolves of Mount McKinley* (D.C.: U.S. Department of the Interior, 1944), p. 12.

Chapter 3. Threats Old and New

1. Barry Holstun Lopez, *Of Wolves and Men* (New York: Simon & Schuster, 1978), pp. 206–208.

2. "Gray Wolves in the Northeastern United States," *U.S. Fish and Wildlife Service*, n.d., <http://midwest.fws.gov/wolf/ne/northeast.htm> (May 23, 2002).

3. Lopez, p. 177.

4. Ibid., p. 183.

5. Ibid., p. 187.

6. North Cascades National Park Interpretive Staff, *North Cascades National Park*, November 19, 1998, <http://www.nps.gov/noca/wolf.htm> (May 23, 2002).

Chapter 4. A Fierce Green Fire

1. Aldo Leopold, *A Sand County Almanac* (New York: Oxford University Press, 1968), p. 130.

2. Ibid., pp. 130–132.

3. L. David Mech, *The Wolf: The Ecology and Behavior of an Endangered Species* (Minneapolis: University of Minnesota Press, 1981), pp. 335–336.

4. "Gray Wolf: (Canis lupus)," *U.S. Fish and Wildlife Service*, June 1998, <http://species.fws.gov/bio_gwol.html> (May 23, 2002).

5. "History and Evolution of the Endangered Species Act of 1973," *U.S. Fish and Wildlife Service*, n.d., <http://endangered.fws.gov/esasum.html> (February 10, 2001).

Chapter 5. The Return of the Wolf

1. Yellowstone National Park, "Yellowstone National Park Facts," n.d., <http://www.nps.gov/yell/technical/yellfact.htm> (May 4, 2001).

2. Thomas McNamee, *The Return of the Wolf to Yellowstone* (New York: Henry Holt & Company, 1997), p. 134.

3. U.S. Fish and Wildlife Service, "News Release," July 11, 2000, <http://www.r6.fws.gov/pressrel/00-18.htm> (March 6, 2001).

4. Ibid.

5. Jeffery Kluger, "The Big (not so bad) Wolves of Yellowstone." *Time*, January 19, 1998, pp. 24–25.

6. U.S. Fish and Wildlife Service, "News Release," July 11, 2000, <http://www.r6.fws.gov/pressrel/00-18.htm> (March 6, 2001).

7. U.S. Fish and Wildlife Service, "Red Wolf, (Canis rufus)," n.d., <http://species.fws.gov/bio_rwol.html> (May 4, 2001).

8. U.S. Fish and Wildlife Service, "Welcome to the Mexican Wolf Recovery Program," n.d., <http://mexicanwolf.fws.gov/> (August 17, 2001).

9. U.S. Fish and Wildlife Service, "Kids Fact Sheet," *Mexican Gray Wolf Web Site*, n.d., <http://mexicanwolf.fus.gov/kids/kidfact.htm> (August 2, 2002).

Further Reading

Askins, Renee. *Shadow Mountain: A Memoir of Wolves, a Woman and the Wild.* New York: Doubleday, 2002.

Green, Jen. *Wolves.* New York: Anness Publishing, Inc., 2001.

Harrington, Fred H. *The Gray Wolf.* New York: The Rosen Publishing Group, Inc., 2002.

———. *The Red Wolf.* New York: The Rosen Publishing Group, Inc., 2002.

Julivert, Maria A. *The Fascinating World of Wolves.* Hauppauge, N.Y.: Barron's Educational Series, Inc., 1996.

Kavanagh, James. *Wildlife of Denali National Park.* Blaine, Wash.: Waterford Press, 1999.

McNamee, Thomas. *The Return of the Wolf to Yellowstone.* New York: Henry Holt, 1997.

Mech, L. David. *The Way of the Wolf.* Stillwater, Minn.: Voyageur Press, 1991.

Murie, Adolph. *The Wolves of Mount McKinley.* Washington: U.S. Department of the Interior, 1944.

Parker, Barbara Keevil. *North American Wolves.* Minneapolis, Minn.: The Lerner Publishing Group, 1997.

Smith, Roland. *Journey of the Red Wolf.* New York: Penguin Putnam Books for Young Readers, 1996.

Swinburne, Stephen R. *Once a Wolf: How Wildlife Biologists Fought to Bring Back the Gray Wolf.* New York: Houghton Mifflin Company, 2001.